Phonics

hens
hop

SCHOLASTIC

Published in the UK by Scholastic Education, 2022

Scholastic Distribution Centre, Bosworth Avenue,
Tournament Fields, Warwick, CV34 6UQ

Scholastic Ireland, 89E Lagan Road, Dublin Industrial Estate,
Glasnevin, Dublin, D11 HP5F

www.scholastic.co.uk

2 3 4 5 6 7 8 9 2 3 4 5 6 7 8 9 0 1

A CIP catalogue record for this book is available from the
British Library.

ISBN 978-1407-18406-7

This Book was printed by Leo Paper Products Ltd, Heshan Astros
Printing Limited, XuanTan Temple Industrial Zone, Gulao Town,
Heshan City, Guangdong Province, China.

The book is made of materials from well-managed,
FSC®-certified forests and other controlled sources.

MIX
Paper from
responsible sources
FSC
www.fsc.org   FSC® C020056

Author
Wendy Jolliffe

Editorial team
Robin Hunt, Kate Pedlar

Design team
Dipa Mistry, Andrea Lewis and Andrew Magee Design

Illustration
Diego Vaisberg / Advocate Art

Contents

Phonics in the early years

This book will help your child to learn about the sounds of our language, which form a vital building block for learning to read and spell. Try to ensure that these activities are kept short and are seen as fun, stopping as soon as your child is tired. Talking to your child as she or he does the activities is important too; hearing and saying the sounds is key to their understanding.

What is phonics?

Phonics refers to an approach that focuses on the sounds of our language and how these can be mapped to letters to help with reading and writing. All schools have a focus on phonics from Nursery onwards.

Children will learn phonics systematically when they start school, but you can help your child make a good start by encouraging them to hear and identify individual sounds. It is important to make this fun. Some examples of games you can play include:

- I hear with my little ear: This is like the familiar games of 'I spy' except you hear the sound instead of looking for things that begin with a letter. For example, say: 'I hear with my little ear something beginning with "ffff"', placing emphasis on the sound.

Note that many sounds can be stretched, such as **m**, **s**, **f**, **l**, **r**, **n**, **v**, and **z**, for example 'mmm' or 'sss', which can help children in the beginning to identify individual sounds. Where you can't stretch the sound, as in **b**, try to avoid saying 'buh' and keep the 'uh' as short as possible, emphasising the **b**.

- Letter races: This could be a fun outdoor activity. You will need magnetic letters and a magnetic board. Place your chosen letters and the board a few metres apart. Call out a sound. The child has to find the letter and run to put it on the board. As you progress you can begin to say short words, such as 'cat', for your child to find all the letters and place on the board.

- Matching rhymes: Here you can have fun saying words that rhyme, such as 'cat', 'hat', 'pat', 'rat', 'sat'. Rhyming is an important part of beginning to identify sounds. You may like to teach your child the well-known song: 'There's a fox in a box in my little bed'. You'll find examples online, for instance:

'There's a fox in a box in my little bed, my little bed, my little bed.
There's a fox in a box in my little bed and there isn't much room for me.'

Continue the song, making up further verses, such as 'There's a snake in a cake in my little bed, my little bed, my little bed…' or 'There's a giraffe in a scarf in my little bed…'.

Ensure all the emphasis on phonics is accompanied by lots of opportunities to share the wonderful world of children's books with your child, so that they see reading as a real pleasure.

How to use this book

In this book, you will find activities for the following sounds: **m**, **g**, **o**, **c/k**, **u**, **r**, **h**, **b**, **f**, **l**, **j**, **v**, **w**, **x**, **y**, **z**, **qu**. The book follows on from *Early Phonics* which focuses on the sounds: **s**, **a**, **t**, **p**, **i**, **n**, **e**, **d**. Together, the books explore the sounds that form the basis for most phonics programmes.

The sounds covered in this book can be made into short words such as 'rub', 'fog', 'rock' and 'stop'. This is important as children need to blend the sounds together to make words once they can hear and say the sounds correctly. In summary, the key for each sound is to:

- hear the sound (help your child to hear it correctly)
- say the sound (help your child to say the sound correctly)
- read the sound (help your child to read the sound correctly)
- write the sound (help your child to write the letter corresponding to the sound).

Try to do lots of oral activities that emphasise the first sound in a word. For example, when you are shopping, you might say: 'some ssssoap', 'floppy ffffish', emphasising the first sound and saying words together that begin with the same sound.

This book provides two pages of activities for each of the key sounds. To help encourage your child, you will find a certificate on page 40 to display when they have completed all the activities. Children can also colour or circle a face to show how hard they found each activity.

Find a quiet space to look at the book with your child; preferably away from other distractions. Interacting is important, as is offering lots of praise for attempts.

 When  appears, read the phrases and perform the actions. Emphasise the sounds in each phrase (e.g. monkeys marching up mountains). Ask your child to join in and repeat until they are confident with the sounds and the actions. A red 'Notes' box on each page also offers extra guidance for parents and carers working with their child.

A minibook, *Rocks in the Fog*, is available online for your child to practise reading the sounds he or she has learned. Reading a book with new words is a great achievement. Make sure you make it enjoyable, supporting your child and practising it so they can eventually read it independently.

Visit www.scholastic.co.uk/FLP35 to download *Rocks in the Fog*. You will also find instructions showing you how to make the printed pages into a minibook, a full set of answers to the activities in this book and a copy of the certificate.

Sound m

 Say the sound **m** and do a funny march like a monkey.

monkeys march up mountains

Draw <u>lines</u> to put the things that begin with **m** on the mountain.

Notes: Help your child to find the things that begin with the sound **m**. Say the words, emphasising the sound **m**.

Can you find five things beginning with **m** hidden in the mountain? Put a circle around them.

Write the letter **m** below.

Notes: Help your child to find and say the objects that begin with the sound **m**.

How did you do? 🙂 🙁 **7**

Sound g

 Say the sound **g**, giggle and point to a girl.

girls giggle with goats

Circle the animals that begin with the sound **g**.

Notes: Help your child to identify the animals; then find the animal names that begin with the sound **g**.

Say the sound **g**. Find the leaves with things beginning with **g**. Put a circle around each one.

Write the letter **g**.

Notes: Help your child to find and say the words that begin with the sound **g**.

How did you do?

9

Sound o

 Say the sound **o**. Wave your arms around like an octopus and try to balance on one leg.

octopuses on oranges

Circle the things that begin with **o**.

Notes: Help your child to say the sound **o**, like the one in 'otter' and then find the objects that begin with **o**.

The octopus is catching things that begin with **o**.
Can you find them? Put a (circle) around each one.

Write the letter **o**.

○ ○ ○ ○

**Notes:** Help your child to find and say the objects that begin with **o**.

How did you do? ☺ ☹ **11**

Sound k

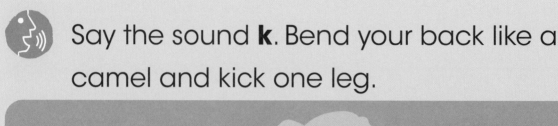 Say the sound **k**. Bend your back like a camel and kick one leg.

camels kick cakes

Colour the rugs that have objects beginning with the sound **k**, written as **c** or **k**.

Notes: Help your child to find and say the words that begin with a **k** sound. Explain that we can write this sound in two ways: **c** and **k**. You can help your child tell the difference by calling these 'curly **c**' and 'kicking **k**'.

Circle the words beginning with c or k.

Write the letters c and k.

Notes: Help your child to find and say the words that begin with **c** or **k**.

How did you do?   😊 😕   **13**

Sound u

 Say the sound **u** and pretend to hold an umbrella and jump.

umbrellas and uncles jump

Colour the umbrellas that have words beginning with **u**.

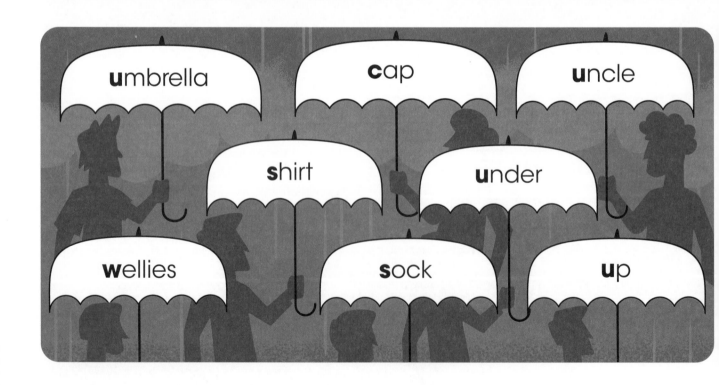

umbrella **c**ap **u**ncle

shirt **u**nder

wellies **s**ock **u**p

14

Draw <u>lines</u> from the letter **u** to the pictures that start with that sound.

Write the letter **u**.

Notes: Help your child to find and say the words that begin with the sound **u**.

How did you do? 🙂 😐 **15**

Sound r

 Say the sound **r** and pretend to be a rabbit running on the spot.

rabbits run and rest

Help the rabbits find their way home. Draw a <u>line</u> from each rabbit to a word that starts with the **r** sound.

rat   ring   bat   top

fox   rabbit   run   rest

Notes: Help your child to spot words beginning with **r**. Say the sound **r** and read the words.

Chase the rabbit around the track. Put a circle around the things that begin with **r**.

Write the letter **r**.

r r r

Notes: Help your child to find and say the words that begin with the sound **r**.

How did you do?

Sound h

Say the **h** sound as you hop and squawk like a hen.

hopping happy hens

Tick (✔) the hen houses that show things beginning with **h**.

Notes: Help your child to spot words beginning with **h**. Say the sound **h** and read the words.

Help the hens hop onto words that begin with **h**.
Cross out (✗) the words that do not begin with **h**.

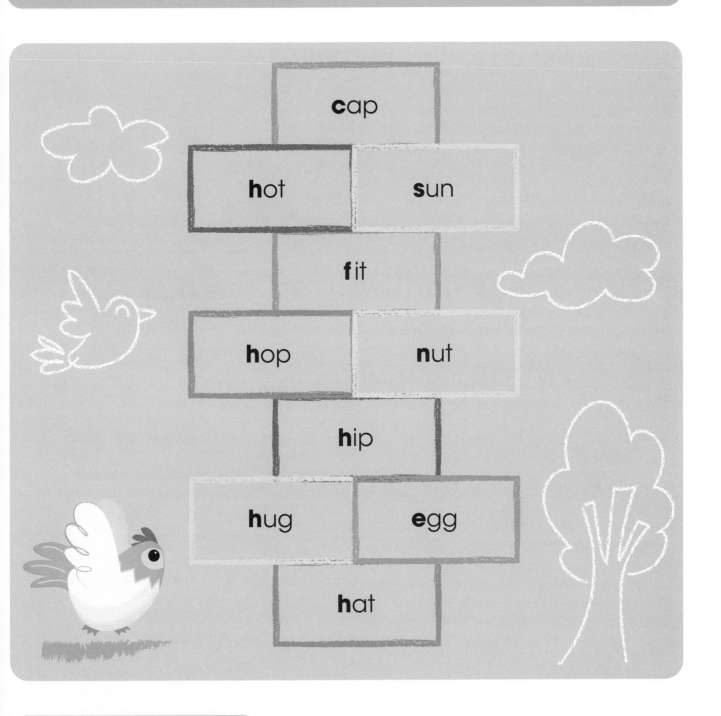

cap

hot　　　sun

fit

hop　　　nut

hip

hug　　　egg

hat

Write the letter **h**.

h h h

Notes: Help your child to find and say the words that begin with the sound **h**.

How did you do?　☺　☹　**19**

Sound b

Say the sound **b**. Pretend to sit on a bus and jump up to ring the bell.

boys and bells on the bus

Play bat and ball. Draw <u>lines</u> to join the bats to the words that begin with **b**.

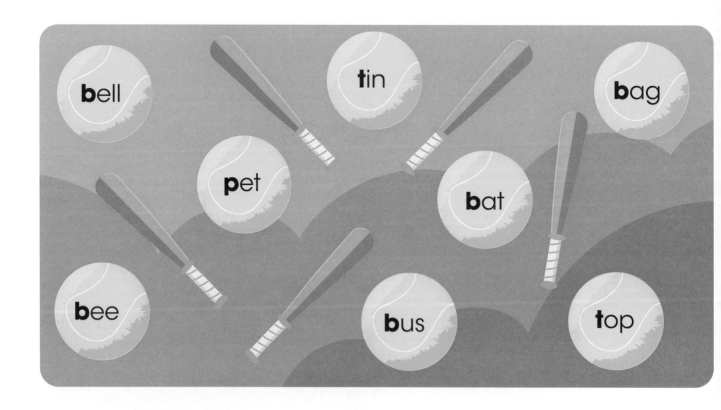

Notes: Help your child to spot words beginning with **b**. Say the sound **b** and read the words.

How many goals can you score? Draw <u>lines</u> from the things that begin with **b** to the net.

Write the letter **b**.

How did you do?

21

Sound f

 Say the sound **f** and flap your arms like a fish.

five floppy fish

Catch the words that begin with **f**. Draw <u>lines</u> to join the rod to the fish.

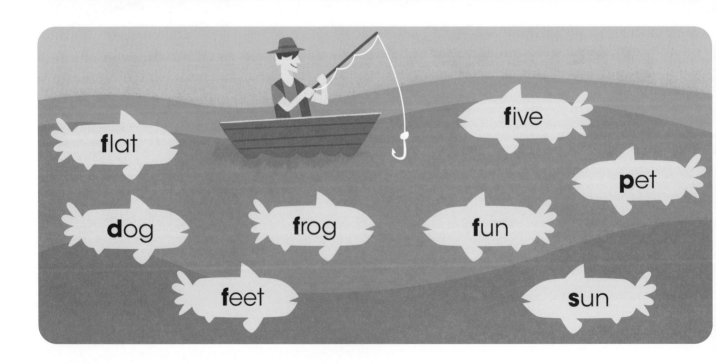

flat

five

pet

dog

frog

fun

feet

sun

Notes: Help your child to spot words beginning with **f**. Say the sound **f** and read the words.

Circle the things on the rocks that begin with **f**.

Write the letter **f** below.

f f f

Notes: Help your child to find and say
the words that begin with the sound **f**.

How did you do?   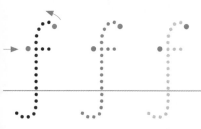   **23**

Sound l

 Say the sound **l** and pretend to lick a lolly.

lick a lolly

Find all the things beginning with **l**. Put a circle around each one.

Notes: Help your child to find and say the words that begin with the sound **l**.

Colour the leaves with words that begin with l.

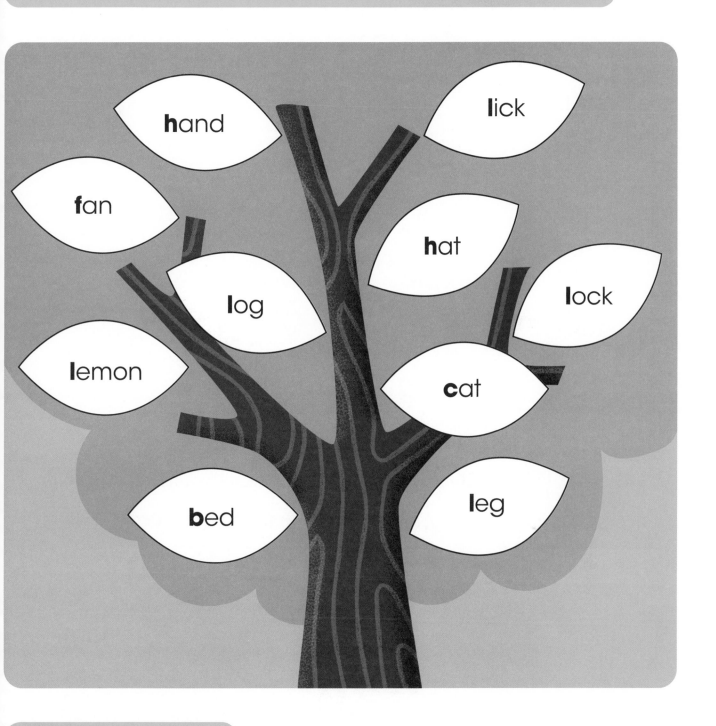

hand
lick
fan
hat
log
lock
lemon
cat
bed
leg

Write the letter l.

l l l

Notes: Help your child to spot words beginning with l. Say the sound l and read the words.

How did you do?

25

Sound j

 Say the sound **j**. Pretend to hold a jug with jelly that wobbles.

jelly jiggles in the jug

The jelly has gone all over the floor! Colour all the pieces that have words beginning with **j** on them.

jug

jam

jet

bed

nest

jar

egg

top

Notes: Help your child to spot words beginning with **j**. Say the sound **j** and read the words.

Fill the jug with **j** sounds. Draw <u>lines</u> from the jug to things that begin with **j**.

Write the letter **j**.

j j j

Notes: Help your child to find and say the words that begin with the sound **j**.

How did you do?  27

Sound v

 Say the sound **v**. Pretend to wipe spilt vinegar off your top.

vinegar on the vest

Colour the vests with words which begin with **v**.

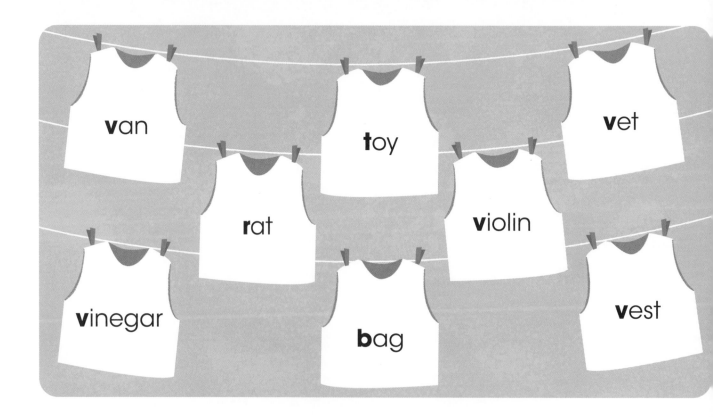

Notes: Help your child to spot words beginning with **v**. Say the sound **v** and read the words.

Help the van to get home. Draw a <u>line</u> along the road that has things beginning with **v** on it.

Write the letter **v**.

v v v

Notes: Help your child to find and say the words that begin with the sound **v**.

How did you do? :) :| **29**

Sound w

 Say the sound **w**, circle arms around and say 'whoosh'.

water wheels went whoosh

Stop things falling in the water. Circle all the things that begin with **w**.

Notes: Help your child to find and say the words that begin with the sound **w**.

30

Can you write the correct letter at the start of each of the words below?

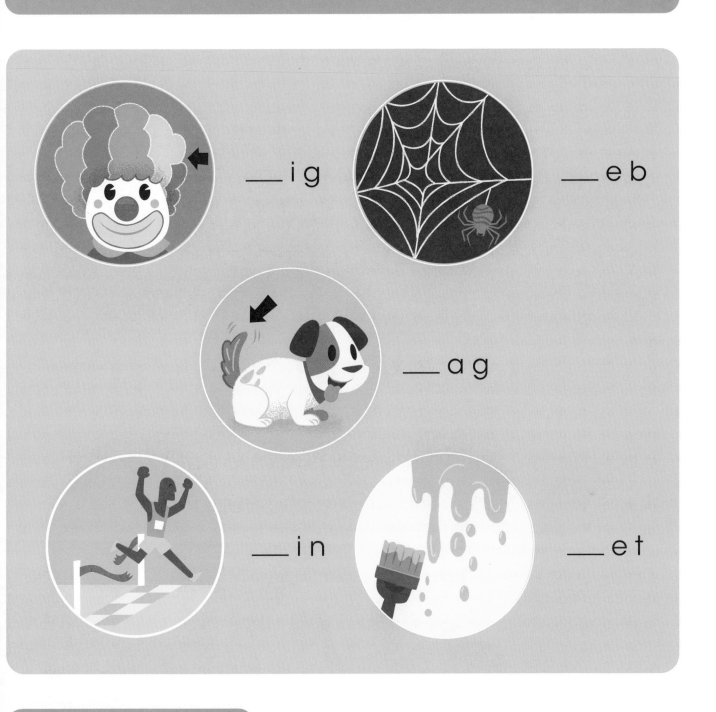

___ i g

___ e b

___ a g

___ i n

___ e t

Write the letter **w**.

W W W

Notes: Help your child to say the sound **w**, write the letter and say the words.

How did you do? ☺ ☹ **31**

Sound x

 Say the sound **x** (**ks**) and pretend to sit on a box.

fox in a box

Stop the fox eating the eggs. Cross out (**✗**) all the eggs with things that have the sound **x** (**ks**).

Notes: Help your child to say **ks** which is the sound that the letter **x** makes. Help them to find the words that contain the sound **x**. This time they will need to look at all the letters in the words.

Circle the pictures with the sound **x** (**ks**).

Write the letter **x**.

x x x

Notes: Help your child to find and say the words that begin with the sound **x** (**ks**).

How did you do?

33

Sound y

 Say the sound **y** and shout 'yum, yum', rubbing your tummy.

yell for yummy yoghurt

The yoghurt monster eats things beginning with **y**. Can you help find them? Circle each one.

Notes: Help your child to find and say the words that begin with the sound **y**.

Can you find the words that begin with **y**? Draw a <u>line</u> to put them inside the big letter **y**.

yes

van

yak

jug

yell

box

yolk

hat

Write the letter **y**.

Notes: Help your child to find and say the words that begin with the sound **y**.

How did you do?

Sound z

 Say the sound **z**, gallop around and make a buzzing noise.

zebras buzz in zoos

Can you help the zebra find his way? Colour the path with things that begin with **z**.

Notes: Help your child to find and say the words that begin with the sound **z**.

Help the bees that are buzzing, looking for words beginning with **z**. Colour them yellow.

zip

jam

zero

bee

zoo

log

zebra

zig-zag

Write the letter **z**.

Notes: Help your child to find and say the words that begin with the sound **z**.

How did you do?

37

Sound qu

 Say the sound **qu** (**kw**). Stand up straight, as if you're waiting in a queue.

queue for a queen

What's in the queue? Cross out (**✗**) the things that don't begin with **qu** (**kw**).

Notes: Help your child to say the sound **qu**, which is a blend of 'k' and 'w' as 'q' in English is nearly always followed by 'u', making the sound **kw**. Children at this age do not need to know this and just learn to recognise the sound **qu**.

Find the words that begin with **qu**. Put a circle around them.

quiz

pen

quad

cake

queen

question

ring

quilt

Write the letters **qu**.

Notes: Help your child to find and say the
words that begin with the sound **qu** (**kw**).

How did you do?

First Learning

★ ★ ★ ★ ★

Certificate

Well done!

You have completed
First Learning Phonics

This certificate is awarded to:

....

Age: ....

Date: ....